WITH LOVE

MW00915358

To

_____

FROM

_____

L♥VE

Loving you was one of the best decisions of my life

love

COUPON
valid for:

Candle Lit Dinner

NO expiry * Non transferable * CAN BE REDEEMED ONLY ONCE

COUPON
valid for:

Full Body Massage

NO EXPIRY * NON TRANSFERABLE * CAN BE REDEEMED ONLY ONCE

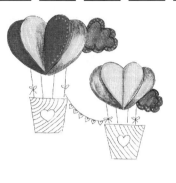

COUPON

valid for:

Slow Dance With Me

NO expiry * Non transferable * CAN BE REDEEMED ONLY ONCE

COUPON
valid for:

UnBirthday Day

NO expiry * Non transferable * CAN BE REDEEMED ONLY ONCE

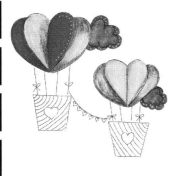

COUPON
valid for:

Relaxing Bubble Bath

NO expiry * Non transferable * CAN BE REDEEMED ONLY ONCE

COUPON
valid for:

Anywhere, Anytime

NO EXPIRY * NON TRANSFERABLE * CAN BE REDEEMED ONLY ONCE

COUPON
valid for:

Breakfast in Bed

NO expiry * Non transferable * CAN BE REDEEMED ONLY ONCE

COUPON
valid for:

Yes All Day

NO expiry * Non transferable * CAN BE REDEEMED ONLY ONCE

COUPON
valid for:

A Fantasy Fulfilled

NO EXPIRY * NON TRANSFERABLE * CAN BE REDEEMED ONLY ONCE

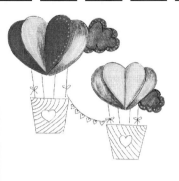

COUPON
valid for:

Win An Argument

NO expiry * Non transferable * can be redeemed only once

COUPON
valid for:

Control The Remote

NO expiry * Non transferable * CAN BE REDEEMED ONLY ONCE

COUPON
valid for:

One Hour Of Role Play

NO expiry * Non transferable * CAN BE REDEEMED ONLY ONCE

COUPON
valid for:

New Position

NO EXPIRY * NON TRANSFERABLE * CAN BE REDEEMED ONLY ONCE

COUPON
valid for:

Cuddling Session

NO EXPIRY * NON TRANSFERABLE * CAN BE REDEEMED ONLY ONCE

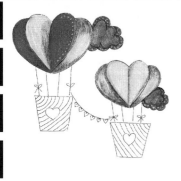

COUPON
valid for:

Netflix & Chill

NO expiry * Non transferable * CAN BE REDEEMED ONLY ONCE

COUPON

valid for:

Naughty Wish

NO expiry * Non transferable * CAN BE REDEEMED ONLY ONCE

COUPON
valid for:

Movie Date Night

NO expiry * Non transferable * CAN BE REDEEMED ONLY ONCE

COUPON
valid for:

Night Out

NO expiry * Non transferable * can be redeemed only once

COUPON
valid for:

Homemade Dinner

NO expiry * Non transferable * CAN BE REDEEMED ONLY ONCE

COUPON
valid for:

The Naked Chef

NO expiry * Non transferable * can be redeemed only once

COUPON

valid for:

Romantic Picnic

NO EXPIRY * NON TRANSFERABLE * CAN BE REDEEMED ONLY ONCE

COUPON
valid for:

Quickie

NO expiry * Non transferable * CAN BE REDEEMED ONLY ONCE

COUPON

valid for:

Last Word In An Argument

NO expiry * Non transferable * CAN BE REDEEMED ONLY ONCE

COUPON
valid for:

Road trip

NO EXPIRY * NON TRANSFERABLE * CAN BE REDEEMED ONLY ONCE

COUPON

valid for:

Get Out Of Jail Free

NO expiry * Non transferable * CAN BE REDEEMED ONLY ONCE

COUPON
valid for:

Lingerie Day

NO EXPIRY * NON TRANSFERABLE * CAN BE REDEEMED ONLY ONCE

COUPON
valid for:

No Chores Day

NO expiry * Non transferable * CAN BE REDEEMED ONLY ONCE

COUPON
valid for:

I Grant You 3 Wishes

NO EXPIRY * NON TRANSFERABLE * CAN BE REDEEMED ONLY ONCE

COUPON
valid for:

Night Out Without Kids

NO expiry * Non transferable * CAN BE REDEEMED ONLY ONCE

COUPON
valid for:

King For One Day

NO expiry * Non transferable * CAN BE REDEEMED ONLY ONCE

COUPON
valid for:

R—Rated Bedroom Time

NO EXPIRY * NON TRANSFERABLE * CAN BE REDEEMED ONLY ONCE

COUPON
valid for:

Surprise Date

NO EXPIRY * NON TRANSFERABLE * CAN BE REDEEMED ONLY ONCE

COUPON
valid for:

Strip Poker Game

NO expiry * Non transferable * CAN BE REDEEMED ONLY ONCE

COUPON
valid for:

69 Time

NO expiry * Non transferable * CAN BE REDEEMED ONLY ONCE

COUPON
valid for:

Morning sex

NO EXPIRY * NON TRANSFERABLE * CAN BE REDEEMED ONLY ONCE

COUPON
valid for:

Shopping spree

NO EXPIRY * NON TRANSFERABLE * CAN BE REDEEMED ONLY ONCE

COUPON
valid for:

Quickie in public place

NO EXPIRY * NON TRANSFERABLE * CAN BE REDEEMED ONLY ONCE

COUPON
valid for:

Naughty game of choice

NO EXPIRY * NON TRANSFERABLE * CAN BE REDEEMED ONLY ONCE

COUPON

valid for:

Skirt + no panties day

NO EXPIRY * NON TRANSFERABLE * CAN BE REDEEMED ONLY ONCE

COUPON
valid for:

Extra Long ForePlay

NO expiry * Non transferable * CAN BE REDEEMED ONLY ONCE

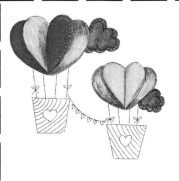

COUPON
valid for:

Wild Card

NO expiry * Non transferable * can be redeemed only once

COUPON
valid for:

Shower for Two

NO EXPIRY * NON TRANSFERABLE * CAN BE REDEEMED ONLY ONCE

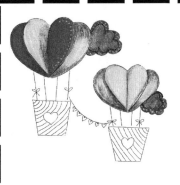

COUPON
valid for:

Fun with Chocolate

NO expiry * Non transferable * CAN BE REDEEMED ONLY ONCE

COUPON
valid for:

Fun Night

NO EXPIRY * NON TRANSFERABLE * CAN BE REDEEMED ONLY ONCE

COUPON
valid for:

Your Wish

_____

NO EXPIRY * NON TRANSFERABLE * CAN BE REDEEMED ONLY ONCE

COUPON
valid for:

Your Wish

_____

NO EXPIRY * NON TRANSFERABLE * CAN BE REDEEMED ONLY ONCE

COUPON
valid for:

Your Wish

_____

NO EXPIRY * NON TRANSFERABLE * CAN BE REDEEMED ONLY ONCE

COUPON
valid for:

Your Wish

_____

NO EXPIRY * NON TRANSFERABLE * CAN BE REDEEMED ONLY ONCE

COUPON
valid for:

Your Wish

NO EXPIRY * NON TRANSFERABLE * CAN BE REDEEMED ONLY ONCE

COUPON
valid for:

Your Wish

_____

NO expiry * Non transferable * can be redeemed only once

Made in the USA
Columbia, SC
19 December 2024

49950225R00057